ALDEN NOWLAN

EARLY POEMS

Acknowledgement and Textual Note

The poems collected in this volume were originally published in *The Rose and the Puritan* (Fiddlehead Poetry Books, 1958), *A Darkness in the Earth* (Hearse Chapbooks, 1958), *Wind in a Rocky Country* (Emblem Books, 1960) *Under the Ice* (Ryerson, 1961), *The Things Which Are* (Contact Press, 1962), and *Five New Brunswick Poets* (Fiddlehead Poetry Books, 1962). This order of publication has been maintained. Poems which appeared in more than one of these collections have been printed in the place of their first appearance and omitted from later sections. These poems, with the collections in which they first appear, followed by the collections in which they were republished, are: in *The Rose and the Puritan*, "A Letter to My Sister" (*Under the Ice*), "A Night Hawk Fell With a Sound Like a Shudder" (*Under the Ice*), "Two Strangers" (*Under the Ice*); in *Wind in a Rocky Country*, "Summer" (entitled "Poem" in *Under the Ice*); in *Under the Ice*, "Therese" (Five New Brunswick Poets); and in *The Things Which Are*, "Sometimes" (*Five New Brunswick Poets*), "The Shack Dwellers" (*Five New Brunswick Poets*), "November 11" (*Five New Brunswick Poets*), "The Genealogy of Morals" (*Five New Brunswick Poets*), "Daisies" (*Five New Brunswick Poets*) and "Fired" (*Five New Brunswick Poets*). Although no attempt has been made to consult the manuscripts of the poems, obvious misprints in the published versions have been corrected without comment.

Published by Fiddlehead Poetry Books, Fredericton, N.B., with the assistance of the University of New Brunswick, the New Brunswick Department of Historical and Cultural Resources, and the New Brunswick Bicentennial Commission.

Cover design by Alexander McGibbon, photograph ("Country Music") by R.E. Balch

Canadian Cataloguing in Publication Data

Nowlan, Alden, 1933-83
Early poems

ISBN 0-86492-019-9 $20.00 hardbound.
I. Title.

PS8527.084E27 1983   C811'.54   C83-098935-8
PR9199.3.N68E27 1983

40,839

Preface

When I think of Alden Nowlan, I see a man in a chair. A massive bearded man with an intensely mobile face, a face registering unquenchable mental energy, laughter and anger bursting from it, in conversations that went on into the small hours of the morning. With his death, I feel the loss of a presence, of a presiding genius in the old sense. Something of the spirit of our place, a spirit we as writers and students of poetry here drew from, has gone. But when I go back to his written words, to his poems, I find that spirit fiercely alive still.

His coming to live among us here in Fredericton in 1968 seems in retrospect a natural culmination of his career, his assuming the role of writer-in-residence not just to a university but to a province. He was destined to be, I think, not just a poet, a journalist, a writer of stories and plays, but a conscience, for us and for our times. He spoke not only to us but for us, as all great writers do.

In 1952, Alden Nowlan, still only nineteen, came to New Brunswick to begin his professional career, as a journalist with *The Hartland Observer*. In the years that followed, he began sending out his poems to little magazines, mostly in the U.S.. Through these he became aware of another poet, Fred Cogswell, a native of his adopted county. A correspondence and a friendship began, which culminated in 1958 with Fred's publishing as his fourth Fiddlehead Poetry Book *The Rose and the Puritan*, a pamphlet containing sixteen poems. By the time he left Hartland for Saint John in 1963 to work for the *Telegraph-Journal*, Alden had published four more books, two of them substantial. These were *A Darkness in the Earth*, *Wind in a Rocky Country*, *Under the Ice* and *The Things Which Are*. Taken together, they represent an astounding body of work from a poet thirty years old.

And this is what the present volume has done—taken these five books together. Before Alden's death, Peter Thomas had approached him with the idea of reprinting the poems in the first two books along with a selection of Reg Balch's photographs. This was to be an appropriate project for the province's Bicentennial. Alden was enthusiastic, and the planned volume was well under way at the time of his death. That event caused his editor to reconsider. What would have been a beautiful but small book appropriate to one occasion now seemed inadequate as a memorial to the dead poet himself. When Peter looked further into the early work, the work reflecting Alden's Nova Scotia childhood and his years in rural New Brunswick, and found so many poems long out-of-print and unavailable to readers, his immediate impulse was to enlarge the proposed book to the proportions you find here. In its original state, it would have been an eloquent tribute; in its present state, it seems to us to be more fitting, a juster portion of a great man's estate offered now to those he loved and who loved him.

Robert Gibbs

CONTENTS

FIVE NEW BRUNSWICK POETS

LIST OF PHOTOGRAPHS

THE ROSE AND THE PURITAN

The Brothers and the Village

The neighbours, in a Sunday meeting mood,
Would roll sweet bits of pity on their tongues
And wonder gravely how the honest Browns
Could breed so little virtue in their sons.

For Jimmie whimpered when he saw a crow
Come down in answer to a classmate's rock,
And fondled roses like a foolish girl,
And quoted school-book poets when he talked.

And Tom shaped women with his pocket knife
From bits of wood, beneath a lazy tree,
Or frightened village maids with silly tales
About the beauty of love's ecstasy.

And John, the eldest, once as mad as they,
But now subdued with children, farm and wife,
Threw all his earnings into books and rum —
And cursed the bitter pointlessness of life.

11

A Letter to My Sister

Dearest of strangers: in your separate room
no smoke intrudes, nor howling from the stable;
the bats make crazy circles in the night —
you smile, adjusting napkins on the table.

The haltered horses scream and flaming shingles
come down like bombs upon the yard and yet
even the heat that cracks these windows shall
never disturb the table that you set.

Running with buckets between barn and well,
seeing so little done by all we do,
my gentle love, I cannot quite decide
whether to pity or to envy you.

Hens

Beside the horse troughs, General Grant
swaggered and foraged in the dry manure,
that winter we had twenty-seven hens
graced with white feathers and names of heroes.

Cock of the walk, he took the choicest fodder,
and he was totem, stud and constable
until his comb and spurs were frozen, bled,
and then the hens, quite calmly, picked him dead.

A Night Hawk Fell With a Sound Like a Shudder

A night hawk fell with a sound like a shudder
    and I was suddenly lonely and cold
sitting there on the fence. Because some rabbit
    or likelier a mouse could not grow old?

No, though in any hunt I'm with the quarry
    it was no mouse's agony that I
felt when I heard the rush of a hawk's wings
    fall without warning from the harvest sky.

A Poem to My Mother

I being twelve and scared, my lantern shook,
shrunk to string my stomach knotted,
breathing the sultry mustiness of hay
and dung in the cowbarn,
and the heifer calving.

Ours was a windy country and its crops
were never frivolous, malicious rocks
kicked at the plough and skinny cattle broke
ditch ice for mud to drink and pigs were axed.

Finding the young bull drowned, his shoulders wedged
into a sunken hogshead in the pasture,
I vomited, my mother, yet the flies
around his dull eyes vanished with the kiss
your fingers sang into my hair all night.

Mother, O gentler Christ, O warmest bed,
hearing the wind at bay your heart was milk;
under the crazy quilting of such love,
needles of adoration knit
bandages for my babied eyes; I slept.

14

Sparrow Come in My Door

Sparrow come in my door, and at the window
your wings, hysterical, shall pound the glass
between you and the sky, invisible,
a nothingness that will not let you pass.

When I was seven in the summer kitchen
a bird flew in and all of mother's breath
escaped in one long sigh because she said
a bird invades the house before a death.

Sparrow come in my door, and at the window
be neither omen, prophecy or sign;
pound at the glass you do not know imprisons
you in your loneliness and me in mine.

15

All Down the Morning

All down the morning, women sprinkled crumbs
Of musty laughter, watching Janice Smith
In brazen languor smear her husband's lips
With public kisses, while he glared or blushed.

And when the Sunday village itched in church,
They thought of Janice, hot as Babylon,
Who lured her Jimmie to the porch and bared
His people's blanket-buried secrecies.

Or dancing to the snarl of feline strings,
Each Friday at the school, they leered at jokes
That made obscenities of her taut breasts
Against her startled husband's sweating suit.

For she was city-bred and unaware
That love was bordered by the rumpled quilts
And children bred from duty as the soil
Was ploughed to hide the seed and not for joy.

So taunted by harsh laughter, half-ashamed,
Enraged with rum and manhood late one night,
And shouting like betrayal, Jim came home
To bruise his knuckles on her shameless face.

The Egotist

A gushing carrousel, the cock
Revolved around the axeman's block.

Sweet Christ, he kicked his severed head
And drenched the summer where he bled.

And terrible with pain, the scream
Of blood engulfed his desperate dream —

He knew (and knowing could not die)
That dawn depended on his cry.

Two Strangers

Two strangers, one of whom was I,
who heard another stranger cry,
when walking in a hunted wood
were frightened into lonelihood.

For one, the sheepish blat of death
re-echoed in his lifted breath;
He drummed his heart for that which dies
and (ritualistic) wet his eyes.

For one, the threshing thing in pain
unloosed wild horsemen in his brain;
he tasted in his rearing will
the salty savour of the kill.

And flank to flank in mist and trees,
they burned with their identities —
two strangers thralled by evil art
to seldom meet and never part.

Weakness

Old mare whose eyes
are like cracked marbles,
drools blood in her mash,
shivers in her jute blanket.

My father hates weakness worse than hail;
in the morning
        without haste
he will shoot her in the ear, once,
shovel her under in the north pasture.

Tonight
        leaving the stables,
he stands his lantern on an over-turned water pail,
turns,
        cursing her for a bad bargain,
and spreads his coat
carefully over her sick shoulders.

Cattle Among the Alders

Cattle among the alders
on the hill among the scrub spruce,
cattle black as leather with white
splashes like milk on their shoulders,
feeding in the khaki grass.

The boy shall come for them
the blue legs of his pants
stroking one another with the sound
that leaves make in the wind and he in love
with all the girls in the world
whistling.

And I know him as though
we had wrestled together in the womb,
and his mother
who is like homemade cider
that goes over the tongue like soapy water
and then is warm and comfortable
in the stomach,

And his father
who laughed when the boy got drunk
on fermented molasses
and whipped the pants off him when he forgot
to water the cattle.

Whistling of Birds

Little bells
under the dark water,
ringing in the dark water,
as the tide moves you;
it is near morning
when I hear you,
shivering like flowers,
little bells in the dark water.

Child of Tabu

Shouting the name our parents whispered,
we circled him in the school yard,
winking at one another complacently
when we found we could make him weep.

It was not strange that we hated him,
who was conceived so casually by strangers
in the soft hay and the high noon.

Begotten furtively in the marital night,
beneath the crush of blankets
and the long shame,

we avowed our ancestry
with the ruthless simplicity of children,
offering our gods
a dripping handful of his heart.

Shouting His Love to Strangers

Shouting his love to strangers,
rumpling the hair of deformed children,
shaking the grimy hands of beggars,
whistling at the ugliest of girls
and stopping an evil old woman
to admire her eyes . . .
                        . . . this was the madness of my brother.

I was not surprised when they came for him,
pinioning his arms in canvas . . .
                        . . . rebuking the gay gush of his laughter
                            with the terrible sanity of their faces.

When Like the Tears of Clowns

When like the tears of clowns the rain intrudes
Upon our ordered days and children chant,
Like repetitious birds, their sexless shrill:
My heart crawls lean and lewd, a shrinking thing,
To haylofts where, when I was ten and whipt,
Tall horses swore fidelity and drummed
As wolf-thoughts howled within my punished wrists.

There in the seasoned hay's unsubtle tang
The lash of fleshly pride unleashed my lips

And in a dream I saw the meek bequeathed
Their deep and narrow heritage of earth.

The Rose and the Puritan

He said, the panthers rendez-vous tonight
outside my cubicle, and beasts with wings
are mauling their tremulous meat. I hear
the blatant bellies of ogres, the clack
of rats — a leper peels his putrid hands
of meaningless fingers, giggling. Praise God
for shelter, even such as this.
                                    She said
nothing. He spoke again and louder, hear
the girls in silken sins and jostled hair
who tempt me with castanets, see the lights
that naked boys have aimed from grape-grown hills,
and, listen!, the wily old cannibals
have thought to lure me to their pots with chants
of freedom. Luckily these walls are sound.

And rose said nothing, nothing at all. God
is my refuge, he whimpered suddenly,
even this lightless tomb, this cell, this cage
is preferable to that which shrieks outside —
the world is wind, the winged wind with claws,

But God is there, not here, said rose,
then mute again she turned the key and smiled.

A DARKNESS IN THE EARTH

Hymn

O God of Hainesville, Mattawa and Bath,
feted with raisin juice and leavened bread,
my bare knees bent like boomerangs of wrath
to you, the wind, the knuckles of the dead.

Think for the moment of one blind from birth,
there was just such a darkness in the earth.

O God, only the passionate profane
express such humours as I shared with you,
boxing with my own body, gone insane,
O God only the passionate profane.

Think for the moment of one blind from birth,
there was just such a darkness in the earth.

I saw the crows they hanged to spook the corn
on Sundays, and a girl with yellow hair
whose belly was accursed; and she was torn
by tongs of talk until her bones were bare.

Think for the moment of one blind from birth,
there was just such a darkness in the earth.
Boxing with my own body gone insane,
O God only the passionate profane.

In the Hainesville Cemetery

Not all these stones
belong to death. Here and there
you read something
like
> John Andrew Talbot, 1885 — 1955
> Mary, his wife, 1887 —

and on decoration day
Mary will come here
and put a jam jar of water and tulips
on her own grave.

> The Talbots are people
> who make the beds before breakfast
> and set the breakfast table
> every night before they go to bed.

Sacrament

God, I have sought you as a fox seeks chickens,
curbing my hunger with cunning.
The times I have tasted your flesh
there was no bread and wine between us,
only night and the wind beating the grass.

In Awful Innocence

Machines in awful innocence ordain
The decalogue of static certainties;
Like Newton's universe and Persia's gods
Assume the changelessness of laws.

Listen, I saw a surging thing of steel,
Convinced three cycles always meant a chair,
Inhale a child and twist its pretty neck,
Then sprinkle varnish in its bloodied hair.

After the First Frost

After the first frost,

resting in the cool shadows,
the undisciplined lilac bushes
a green web around her,

old woman in brown stockings,
smelling of wintergreen
a clean burn in my nostrils,
sipping hot milk and ginger,
among the dead lilacs.

Her daughter I knew as a legion of whispers:
how she lay three summers in the hen house,
rocking her simple baby.

And the old woman swept out the hen house with
        spruce boughs,
and built her a hammock from a crazy quilt,
till the baby's head grew
unnatural and huge, and he died.

And the old woman pried him loose from her arms
and laid him on a board between two chairs,
and clothed him in velvet trousers
and a shirt bleached out of flour bags,

and went out to wait in the shadows,
the tilting branches closing around her.

Go

Elizabeth, in your shoes with tartan laces,
gather your books and go,
running so fast your pony-pig-tail bounces.

Soon all the corridors are dusk, the classes
dismissed. The janitor
mingles with crooked shadows as he passes

through the incredible emptiness and silence
like an abandoned one.
Run, Elizabeth, run!

Blue Ballad

When Janet saw her sister's lips were blue
She came to me and said, if sister sleeps
What is this arctic mood of hers that creeps
Across her cheeks and leaves her kisses blue?

And Janet thought and thought of polar blue,
Of skies when rinsed with rain, of summer seas,
Of Alice gowns, new skirts, and whispered, please
Why does my sister sleep with lips of blue?

And I was loath to think of polar blue,
Of Alpine ice that holds its prey for years
Preserved as if in mockery of tears—
I lied that sister's lips were never blue.

Flossie at School

Five laths in a cotton dress
was christened Flossie
and learned how to cry,
her eyes like wet daisies
behind thick glasses.

She was six grades ahead of me
and wore bangs; the big boys
called her "The Martian",
they snowballed her home,
splashed her with their bicycles,
left horse dung in her coat pockets.

She jerked when anyone spoke to her,
and when I was ten
I caught up with her one day
on the way home from school,
and said, Flossie I really like you
but don't let the other kids know I told you,
they'd pick on me, but I do like you,
I really do, but don't tell anybody.
And afterwards I was ashamed
for crying when she cried.

I Saw My Daughter's Mercy Spare

I saw my daughter's mercy spare
The fly that tripped a spider's snare;
I watched her hold the rescued mite
And touch its wings in rapt delight.

And touch its wings in rapt delight,
Embrace its weakness with her eyes,
Caress its foulness with her might,
Like a pig-tailed god of flies.

Like a pig-tailed god of flies,
As she pouted in surprise
At its tickling tries at flight
Before she crushed her fingers tight.

Only the Lazy Boy

Only the lazy boy whose lax guitar
Idled through dusty summer saw her go

With wind in skirts and grasses to the fence,
Over, into the croaking swamp below.

Only the lazy boy was spared the dark
Rumours of how her final day was spent,

And strange in one whose ways were slow with sleep,
Only the lazy boy knew why she went.

Parakeet

The Pentecostal parakeet who speaks,
Like Peter, tongues he cannot understand,
Sits lisping on my thumb, repeats, repeats
With high fidelity, bewhiskered damns.

He says profane, profane, profane and tweet,
Consigns my soul to hell and shakes the flame
Of fire-blue feathers, as a bird might laugh
If birds were laughers; I caress his beak

With tenderest perversity as one
Will pat a small boy's bottom, perhaps, or lift
A cat by furry nape—I say 'how can
So small a bird contain so many damns?'

He glares at me from sullen slits that throb
With hate that only dwarfs and caged things know,
And silent suddenly he pecks and pecks
With rage so mad it tickles in my hand.

Atlantis

No waves ten storeys tall and terrible,
abrupt and hissing as a severed vein,
erased this city. First the rivers spilled
across our outer provinces, and then
there was some talk of dams, but most of us
approved of irrigation, anyhow
the peasants need a bath sometimes, we said,
and later when the swamps began to swell
and gulls were white against the misty sky,
the ancients said almost the same occured
often when they were young, and so of course
we were ashamed to mention things like drips
we heard at night, and someone always laughed
when little men at parties claimed that pools
were rising slowly, slowly in their cellars.

WIND IN A ROCKY COUNTRY

Marian at the Pentecostal Meeting

Marian I cannot begrudge
    the carnival of God,
the cotton candy of her faith
    spun on a silver rod

to lick in bed; a peaked girl,
    neither admired nor clever,
Christ pity her and let her ride
    God's carrousel forever.

Baptism

Along the river, women sing of sin
and girls in dripping dresses dry their hair,
and giggle in the water, half-afraid
of thoughts as high and marvellous as prayer.

The preacher's hands are certain like his faith,
and sweep reborn devotees from the womb
of cleansing water where they hymn in praise
of Him who rose who broke a stronger tomb.

And when they wade, enwrapped in towels, to shore
the girls like damp young angels stop to greet
their younger sisters, whom they bless with tears
and kiss—with new and womanly conceit.

Our Brother Exalted

A hardware salesman, potentate and priest
of Arab brothers, he displays the chain
of sheikdom, ruling all the Mystic East,
encompassed by the hall on Fifth and Main.

Each Monday night he lifts the sacred sword
and orders grocery clerks to drain the blood
of interlopers found without the word
that marks each lawful wearer of the hood.

And when, in arcane ritualistic prose,
he orders closure of the occult tome,
their carpeted Sahara seeks repose,
and they play nickel poker and go home.

Summer

It's summer yet but still the cold
coils through these fields at dusk, the gray Atlantic
haunting the hollows and a black bitch barking
between a rockpile and a broken fence
out on the hill a mile from town where maybe
a she-bear, groggy with blueberries, listens
and the colt, lonesome, runs in crooked circles.

Partnership

Aliens, both like the last survivor
of some lost tribe, the old man drunk
on lotions, his breath like a brothel, the boy
half-certain he's seen a star
fall like a hawk and roll in the dooryard—
each practised
in talking to himself, the weather
or anything else that listens:

the old man teaches
the boy about mermaids;
the boy filches
bay rum and tonics—

the crippled monkey
on the blind dog's back.

Neighbours

Bitch fox stealthy
but the grass betrays you
shivering with impatience;

it is my duty
being neighbourly
to kill you—

my uncle the deacon
questioned God's purposes
in creating you,
chicken thief.

John Sproull
would spit in my eye
if he could see me
wishing you well at his henyard.

Street Corner Idler

His tragedy is that he seems to wait—
idlers should swagger in and entertain!
the tramps in mother's kitchen always paid
mouth organ tunes and stories sad as plays.

They had unfaithful sons and cheating wives
and when they left us it was strangely pleasant
to think of them, full of our beans and bread,
turning beside the gate to thumb their noses.

To Sylvia on her Fourteenth Birthday

Suspicious of the customary oughts,
    the peevish algebra of argument,
I too am pricked by quint-thorned senses, share
    your brittle joys, your skittish discontent.

All royal questions lead to wharves of where,
    zig-zag through seas of why to farther riddles:
philosophers ransack the violin
    until they doubt that anybody fiddles.

Life being various, Goliath falls
    prey to the stone-propelled tribute of love,
sometimes; such singular plurality
    affiliates the tiger and the dove.

To traffick with reality involves
    the risk of shrinkage—shrinkage is to know,
say, that your patron saint was half a rogue
    and, knowing, crow.

Sylvia, truth is vast and more
than two and two are firmly four,
for two and two sometimes will be
an atom of infinity.

You, in your bicycle pants,
torero tight around
the April slenderness of boy-girl legs;
you, whose ambition
is to have sixteen years
and a boy with a motorcycle,
what can I add who love you
neither as father nor lover
but with a love greater
and less than theirs,
being almost impersonal?

At the Fair

Terry and I at the Fair
won everything—
        we filled the car

with green-eyed bears,
black jackasses with red-lined ears
and one old tiger with horsehair
whiskers that tickled

        my neck, there was barely room
        left for us:

we got drenched,
running to the car,
and sat there,
laughing crazily among our queer beasts,

        as the empty Ferris wheel
        went around
        and around
        in the rain.

Clarence Carle

Though Clarence Carle inherited a basement
sufficient for a college or a convent,
he never built upon it, pitched a shack
behind the cellar wall. When I went back
to talk with him he'd tell me how his place
was equal to his means, he was content,
he said, and planned to fill the hole
with dirt and plant potatoes as a fool
could see that that was practical. And yet
his eyes were tortured with an old regret.

I Knew the Seasons Ere I Knew the Hours

I knew the seasons ere I knew the hours;
the Christmas cactus blossomed anytime
after December first and scarlet flowers
fell patiently, in patterns like the blood
from shallow wounds, in mother's russet parlour.

I was once six and so damned lonely
I called love Rover, he had two sad ears,
a black-white checkerboard of face, a nose
for venison, he stole my uncle blind,
was caught and shot and buried in the pasture.

For months I sprinkled daisies over him,
sucking my grief like lemons. Stephanie
shredded the daisies when she punished me
for being born her brother and we wrestled,
crushing the grass like lovers, till our mother
whipt us apart. Eventually the flowers
were laid less for my grief than for that struggle.

Pussywillows in March

Pussywillows beside the full ditches
blossoming in the season
when the last snow
is more soot than crystal,

there are such curious conflicts
in you, joy and sadness,
and a strange loveliness
in your mud-coloured stalks
and the little blossoms
in their leathery pouches
that are exactly
the colour of an old white shirt
that doesn't look clean
no matter how often you wash it.

God Sour the Milk of the Knacking Wench

God sour the milk of the knacking wench
with razor and twine she comes
to sanchion our blond and bucking bull,
pluck out his lovely plumbs.

God shiver the prunes on her bark of chest,
who capons the prancing young.
Let maggots befoul her alive in bed,
and dibble thorns in her tongue.

Poem for the Golden Wedding of my Puritan Grandparents

Their love was sister to the starving deer
and brother to December. Had he called
her "darling" in his annual drunkenness,
(for he got drunk at Christmas) her lean lips
would have recoiled as when she tasted milk
that had gone sour or observed a girl
in little breeches. So he always spoke
of her as the "old lady", "ma" or "Maud".
And in their fifty years they never kissed.

But when he withered of the fanged disease
that ate his vitals till he lived on slop
and sat in silence louder than a groan,
we children marvelled how she sometimes sat
for hours simply staring at his face,
and how before they closed the box she bent
with awful eagerness to pat his hand.

Poem

For Helen and Martha Knox,
Hainesville, New Brunswick

Missionaries to Kenya, 1910-40

The sisters Knox were thirty years in Kenya—
Christ in a cedar chest brought out to smother
bare-naked men, bull gods, eccentric weather,
demented vegetation, the hyena:

Wesleyan gentlewomen having ices,
humming and hemming in a manse rose garden.
Hush, dung-flanked Africa—no serpent jargon!
God has his merciful, if daft, devices.

For Nicholas of all the Russias

Wind in a rocky country and the harvest
meagre, the sparrows eaten, all the cattle
gone with the ragged troopers, winter coming,
mother will starve for love of you and wrapping
newest and least accustomed leave him squalling
out in the hills beside the skulls of foxes,
it cold and snow in the air. Stranger, knocking,
(now in this latter time even the poor
have bread and sleep on straw) what silly rumour
tells me your eyes are yellow and your lips
once rose trout-quick to suck a she-wolf's teats?

Our Lord, his peaked heir and hawk-faced daughters
are gone, although they say one severed finger
was found after the soldiers cleaned the cellar.

UNDER THE ICE

A Poem for Elizabeth Nancy

Emptied from Eden, I look down
into your eyes like caves behind a torrent,
into the blue-green valleys where the cattle
fatten on clover and grow drunk on apples;

into the house asleep and all the curtains
skittish and white as brides (even the wind
meeting their silence, whispers) and I come
into the house with hands that stink from milking,

into this house of candles where my feet
climbing your stairs like laughter leave me standing
before your door, knowing there's no one there,
knowing your room is bare and not much caring.

Beginning

From that they found most lovely, most abhorred,
my parents made me: I was born like sound
stroked from the fiddle to become the ward
of tunes played on the bear-trap and the hound.

Not one, but seven entrances they gave
each to the other, and he laid her down
the way the sun comes out. Oh, they were brave,
and then like looters in a burning town.

Their mouths left bruises, starting with the kiss
and ending with the proverb, where they stayed;
never in making was there brighter bliss,
followed by darker shame. Thus I was made.

Gypsies

Jessie, my cousin, remembers there were gypsies
every spring, cat-eyes in smoky faces,
hair like black butter on leather laces.
Mothers on the high waggons whose babes sucked
flesh on O'Brien Street, I'd be ashamed.
The men stole everything and damned if they didn't
shrug if you caught them—giving back a hen
filched from your own coop like a gift to a peasant.
The little girls danced, their red skirts winking,
their legs were lovely, greasy as drumsticks.
And they kidnapped children. Oh, every child
hoped secretly to be stolen by gypsies.

Refuge at Eight

Darkness, the smell of earth, the smell of apples,
the cellar swallowed me, I dreamt I died,
saw both blind parents mad with guilt and sorrow,
my ghost sardonic. Finally, I cried.

Aunt Jane

Aunt Jane, of whom I dreamed the nights it
      thundered,
was dead at ninety, buried at a hundred.
We kept her corpse a decade, hid upstairs,
where it ate porridge, slept and said its prayers.

And every night before I went to bed
they took me in to worship with the dead.
Christ Lord, if I should die before I wake,
I pray thee Lord my body take.

To Jean

So cold that any house seemed like a fire,
I snapped the lock that was less lock than symbol.
It was a rivet and a twisted wire
and I was seventeen and scared and nimble.

You twenty miles away and with a lover
I broke your empty house and stole its heat.
The stove all cold I pulled a jacket over
my shaking shoulders, slept and found sleep sweet.

Background

Where I come from, the kick of love
recalls the laughter in the throats
of boys who knocked the privy down
before the teacher could get out.

The Belled Deer

There used to be wild deer across the river,
one of them wore a bell and no one knew
its origin and so the legends grew;
grandfather thought no natural brute was ever
as swift as that one was or half so clever.
Though every fall the hunters sought her, told
of bell-sounds like the touch of ice on gold,
they said that mortal hand would kill her never.

Nobody hunts there now; a tracker's snow,
a windless afternoon were once enough
to sweep the orchards with a rifle screen.
They wanted meat, of course, for times were tough,
but there was not a man who had not seen
the belled deer in his sights and let her go.

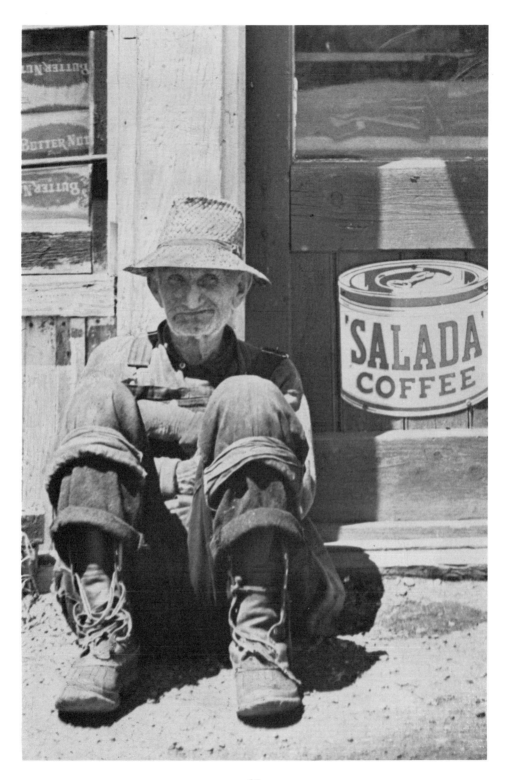

The Coat

My grandmother's boy is dead,
his skull fractured he did not speak
as she knelt down on the dirt road
and wept on his face, her hand under his head.

My grandmother's boy was wild
as the blackbirds in Minard's clearing.
He stood up on the pedals, yodelling;
the wind too seems to ride toward death.

My father took the corduroy coat
of my grandmother's boy and hid
it behind a beam where she found it and came
weeping with it hugged to her breast,
walking slowly under the clothes line
down the pathway beside the woodshed.

There were bloody stains and the stains of mud
almost indistinguishable on the coat,
and her black dress with its red flowers
came like a ghost berating
my father as though he'd killed.
When he took the coat from her
he was so gentle I was amazed. Afterwards
he cursed and poked the coat viciously,
using a stick to crowd it
into the kitchen fire.

Cousins

My cousins, the kind
of family who in another time
and place took to brigandage
for the hell of it,

> so violent they go logging
> or harvesting their meagre acres
> as if they were going on a raid,
> work twelve hours, then hitch-hike to a dance
> in Larchmont or Bennington,
> get drunk as a fiddler's bitch,
> roostering for skirts and fist-fights;

and when one of them
gets a girl in trouble,
which is inevitable,
he marries her,

> it's a point of honour
> with them to treat their wives
> like whores, they talk about bedding
> them as they talk
> about going to the privy,

they are so afraid
of weakness, my cousins
who are not frightened
by boots or tire-irons
behind the dance hall in Bennington
are scared into hilarity and contempt by kisses.

My Father

My father never takes
anything for granted—
food, shelter, sleep,
he is always grateful.

He lives alone now,
when he opens the pantry
he always acts amazed
that there is bacon and flour.

He eats slowly
surprised there's enough
finishes wiping
his plate out with bread.

He is seldom happy
but I never saw a man
so content with small comforts:

wife, children gone
there is nothing left—

I know he could curl up
in his mackinaw
on his own barnfloor
and sleep thankful
at being allowed to rest there.

Testament

If I am sentimental
curse me, it is my inheritance,
what I bequeath
is laughter to the young lovers
of this country where summer
is tense always, a lull between storms,
where even in August
I can sense the snow clouds.
I would have it
so the first time
you are frightened, but not much,
and afterwards when the old janitor
gone crazy with religion
sweeps the snow off the steps
of our three churches, being most careful
with his own, you come awake slowly
and lie quiet for a long time
in the warmth of one another's arms.

Bone Dry and at Jimmie Kelly's

Five dogs, bitch-crazed in the dying mustard,
challenged my car and a black goat
chewed most mournfully at a black coat
drying upon the fence. I said the word

appropriate to such a place and thirst
and Tommy went in quickly and came out
hiding a bottle. Jimmie Kelly cursed
all bitches generally and kicked the goat.

Father

Father, she says, was handsome as a Spaniard,
rode a bay stallion in the Depression
and fed it better than he fed himself.
He was a strict and pious gentleman.

He called me princess even when he paced
his study with the black hypnotic tongue
of the whip licking at his riding boot.
There's not one man like him among the young.

Poem

A silence like a lizard on the tongue,
    quiet that is not peace stalks through the mind,
searching for words in all the empty rooms,
    birds that no wicker cages have confined.

Grim is the shadow of wanton despair,
    icy the rooms where not a bird is crying.
Stop at the window, motionless as mute,
    even the hawk may come, when you've ceased
        trying.

Baptism

In summer-coloured dresses, six young girls
are walking in the river; they look back,
frightened and proud; a choir and a cloud
of starlings sing; in rubber boots and black
frock-coat the preacher bends them separately
under; since the up-rushing stream expands
their skirts as they go down he closes them
each time with gently disapproving hands.

Saturday Night

Every five minutes they turn,
with their tires like sirens,
tusking the dirt up on the creek road,
and drive back through town—

      slowing down on Main Street, manoeuvring
      between the farmers' cars, hooting
      at girls on the pavement who reply
      with little hen movements, laughing, waiting.

The boys sport leather jackets and levis,
but that's their underwear,
the car is their real clothing:
at Taylor's Corner they turn again,
their Hollywood mufflers
making sounds furious, derisive, vulgar—
like a bear growling and breaking wind,

      and roar through Main Street again.

Sunday Afternoon

In the next house they're punishing a child.
Violently too: the boy is being whipped
with something limber that thwacks like applause,
water that's stoned or cotton when it's ripped.

All three are yelling. Though the boy
uses no proscribed idioms, it's plain
he's cursing manfully. But also begging—
defiant yet obsequious in pain.

The mother's inconsistent too, she wants
the boy whipped, obviously, but she hates
the man for beating him. So she exhorts
the son vindictively and still berates

the father's harshness. He a normal man
playing a role he loathes, a prisoner,
expresses his abhorrence of the whole
mess by applying himself to it harder.

The Lodge

Kneeling with fastened wrists before the skull
that's flanked with lamps of salt and alcohol
men are ennobled in fraternity,
swear to submit to sundry mutilitations
should they betray the awesome secrecy
that hides the First Truth like a tasselled curtain:
life is what is but death is fairly certain.

That solemn preface done the new-made peers
undress blindfold and march in bare feet that
have been first drenched with water on a mat
wired for electricity, the cheers
of their new kinsmen roaring in their ears
as they prance goatishly and buck and bleat.

Homebrew

Molasses, oranges and yeast
purchased with promises and mixed at night,
the keg buried in steaming dung
to hasten fermentation, then the wait
for some excuse to fork it out
(a rainy day, the mill not running);
the men in their sawdust-covered denims
sitting on blocks of pressed hay in the barn
and drinking from a single mug, their thumbs
spooning out shreds of hay and frequently
flies and then bolting it, holding their breath,
and spitting afterwards, grunting their pleasure.

At the Lunch Counter

A girl, fifteen perhaps,
licking her finger-tips,
smoothing splotches
of butter and salt
off her blue pants,
cheek muscles rippling.

Nathan who is blind
sidles to the stool beside her.

They talk, he pompously,
she making faces
he can't see,
telling the boys she isn't serious.

I'm Barbara, she says,
blowing her cheeks out,
wrinkling her forehead,
Fred Ward's Barbara.
I have red hair!

She giggles
since her hair is brown
with aluminum
fishes at the temples.

But he can't see.

Then,
she stiffens and frowns
wanting us to go away
so she can be kind.

Rehearsal

So old that every ghost's a friend, he sits
propped up with canes, pelted with schoolboy teasing,
here in our little street and plots his funeral
down to the last amen and finds it pleasing

to choose again the six mane-tossing stallions,
the six pert dandies with their silver handles,
the girls to pitch the hymns like rose-white doves
out of their mouths, over the blessed candles.

The Fynch Cows

The Fynch cows poisoned:
they'd torn the fence down,
gored one another for the befouled weed;
next day they bloated
and their bowels bled,
and they staggered crazily
around the miserly pasture—

John Fynch crying
as he stumbled after them,
with his rifle.

Jack Stringer

Jack Stringer kissed his mother twice a year,
when he came home from Calgary and when
he left again and every year the time
between the kiss of greeting and the kiss
of farewell became briefer, and he went
farther to show his love for her—like going
with her to the Free Baptist Church and smoking
cigarettes in the porch, being polite
to all her friends and smiling gently at
her ignorance; recalling with each kiss
why that first great escape had been such bliss.

Rosemary Jensen

Rosemary Jensen died, to death's surprise,
she'd fought so long to wrench the burning coal
he'd buried in her from her sullen soul,
and there was so much hatred in her eyes.

And all the neighbourhood remarked how hard
Tom Jensen took it; gathered at the grave,
ashamed, faintly disgusted, heard him rave,
were slow to leave him when they reached his yard.

But he went in the house and locked them out
and for the only time in thirty years
drank whiskey in the kitchen, dried his tears,
tumblers of laughter cracking in his throat.

Alex Duncan

He's wanted to go back
since that first fall:
1920 and the frost
rending the crops
with its cold and passionate
Canadian hands.

There's never been enough.
The army worms ate up
the first fare home,
floods took the second,

and the bitch cancer
that he half imagines
to have been some animal
native here, gobbled the third,
eating the woman's breasts.

Four decades away from home
his Scottish tongue
grows broader every year.
One looks for heather
to spring up between his toes.

Sheilah Smith

Awakening as people do in dreams
naked upon the mayor's lawn, not sure
whether the crowd had come to see the fire
or take the sacraments, but certain her
presence was an embarrassment, she first
wept and embraced herself, and then, unable
to make them understand, threw up her arms
and danced—extravagantly—on the table.

Andy Shaw

Three generations (and he loathed them all)
    bought meat from Andy Shaw who clerked for
        Etter,
working six days a week for thirty years,
    hating his job and looking for a better.

He never married and he blamed his wage,
    never went more than twenty miles from town;
and every year came earlier to work,
    cursing the butcher shop that tied him down.

When Charley Etter died his son came home
    to run the store, so Andy got his pay.
Some claim the old man cried, offered to work
    for less—or nothing—if they'd let him stay.

Charlie

For twenty-five cents
or, if properly approached, a dime
he'll chew up a razor blade
crack it between his teeth
and grin at the same time.

Usually, it's the kids
who hire him,
a gang of them
chipping in pennies—their applause
pleases him

as he swallows
thinking how much
blood there is in a dollar.

This Woman's Shaped for Love

This woman's shaped for love, one thinks each breast
might have been grown to fit in a man's hand,
her mouth moulded by constant kisses, and
her legs devised by an evangelist.
She promenades as if her feet were headed
toward an elopement; through the plodding town
her rich posterior lilts up and down—
surely a girl begotten to be bedded.

So boys ache after her and men of age
wish they could have a little while it lasts;
young girls sniff and go home to imitate
her every motion, like enthusiasts.

And nights—her husband kneads in fists of rage
flesh that no human touch can animate.

Warren Pryor

When every pencil meant a sacrifice
his parents boarded him at school in town,
slaving to free him from the stony fields,
the meagre acreage that bore them down.

They blushed with pride when, at his graduation,
they watched him picking up the slender scroll,
his passport from the years of brutal toil
and lonely patience in a barren hole.

When he went in the Bank their cups ran over.
They marvelled how he wore a milk-white shirt
work days and jeans on Sundays. He was saved
from their thistle-strewn farm and its red dirt.

And he said nothing. Hard and serious
like a young bear inside his teller's cage,
his axe-hewn hands upon the paper bills
aching with empty strength and throttled rage.

Steve Johnson's Daughter at His Death

Of course she's sad
still it's a great adventure:
her father dead.

Everyone tries
to say the right thing
and nobody complains—the wet wreath on the door
says this is a special place; death's wings
touched her, but like a caress, death is no angel:
the old man went down like a cat
with a hen on its back.

The neighbours all come
and look at him
lying down in his serge suite—as if he'd ever
lain down in his suit, even sitting
he'd pull the cuffs up to keep the press;
it's one of the things that doesn't matter now.

They look at her too,
she knows it—last night
she refused to come in from the barn,
lay in the haymow listening
to all the people pleading.
Oh, she was sad,
but it was a fine feeling.

Carl

Nobody has ever seen Carl
when he wasn't smiling.

He grins at cats and hydrants
and a huge, wet, collie-like smile
lights up whenever anybody, no matter who,
speaks to him.

When he's hurt
his smile shrinks a little,
pulls its corners in snugly,
but it doesn't go away.

Georgie and Fenwick

Georgie and Fenwick Cranston,
in their thirties and unmarried,
Hainesville calls them old bachelors,
live with their parents on a potato farm,
six miles north of town—
they're afraid of girls.

    Saturday nights,
    in front of the Farmers Store
    some of the girls,
    their little posteriors
    gift-wrapped in Christmas-coloured
    short pants, always stop
    to tease them.

Cecelia Cameron, pressing
so close to Fenwick his overalls
scratch her bare legs, whispers,
Fenwick, do you still love me?

    When she backs away
    her breasts ripple
    under her striped blouse,
    she puts her fists in her pockets,
    tightening her pants,
    tugging them up her thighs,
    she says, Georgie
    do you want to take me home tonight?

And everybody laughs,
except Georgie and Fenwick,
who say nothing,
their mouths open,
their eyes half-shut,
blushing, rocking back and forth
in their gum rubbers. They look
like rabbits frozen
with fear of the gun.

Carl Spicer

My earliest ambition was like Cain's:
to be another and acceptable.
One from my mother's womb spewed out his brains
between my boots, as in the parable.

The Young Rector

The young rector,
an Anglo-Catholic,
is perfectly scrupulous,

but the shepherd
gets lonesome
talking to sheep
even when he loves them,

so he confides in me:
these people are dead,
all they need is someone
to throw dirt over them.
Passionless, stinking, dead.

These thirty minutes
he is the cub lion
tearing at its lamb
making violent gestures
with teeth and shoulders
until he exhausts himself

and can go back
and love them again.

A Duty Call on Paul McCullough His Fifth Year Bedfast

Paul who endures
the weight of a coffin
without its brass splendour
or cushions, astounds me—

his facial skin
looks removable, one imagines
it on the tray
with his dentures
when the skull sleeps.

But he smokes, talks
politics and scandal, and
his wife assures me
eats like a bear.
She chuckles,
eyeing him resentfully.

I wonder if he understands.

Birth

I've seen Christ born, a stranger in the wind,
coughing in an old coat, cornered and blind,
playing the mouth organ; I saw his pay
was nickels and that only if the songs were gay.

Patricia Grey

Somebody loved Patricia Grey enough
    to carve an angel that's stood ninety years
over her grave though cattle and wild deer
    pasture upon her now and no one cares.

This afternoon I stopped to look at her
    among the purple thistles and it seemed
natural that I stooped and kissed her lips
    as though they were not stone but only dreamed.

A Phoebe on the Ground

The heart torn out
encased in feathers
pounding in the hot dust:

this small and smothering
bird overcome
by the smouldering weather.

The Homecoming

They'd never been so long apart before.
So they weren't sure of what to say. He said,
I guess there's not much news, the kids are well.
She nodded. Shyly, they went up to bed.

Blossoms

Reticent and subtle, lovely and full of light,
but sinister too as if a cat's eyes dangled
down from these tawny stalks, this is a weed
—one that does men no good, drawing its life
out of the soil that won't discriminate—
torn up, ploughed under, rooted out, incinerated,
but never beaten, never exterminated.

Walking Home from Work

Ahead a girl
in blue linen shorts,
small beads of sweat
rolling down the backs
of her legs, leaving gray stains
on her wrinkled socks.

On her thigh
a mud-coloured mole
full of moist hairs
keeps time with her step.

It is so hot
I notice every detail
yet have not decided
if her legs are beautiful or not.

John Watching Television

The room is empty except for his mind
which stands on the table like a radioactive platter
pulsating in the impossible confinement
of a mahogany picture frame.

A miracle consists of a violent solution
to an insoluble problem.
The mind absorbs such miracles—love stories
end in a permanent kiss, and crimes
are committed only by criminals,
but the central fact
is that any knot can be untied
by a knife or a pistol shot.

It is not surprising—
any of the great contemplative
saints would understand it perfectly—
that the body is so quiet
in the midst of the miraculous.
He lies still enough
to be asleep, his capacity
for violence filled
by the mind's projected, incandescent platter.

The Gift

"My son sent it," she says. The man-shaped stone
stands in its broken wrappings on the table,
defying measurement: six inches tall,
perhaps, but monstrous too, a brutal bulk
sensed in its attitude. Too starkly human.
"Esquimaux carve them," she explains. Her son.
wrote her from Resolute. She laughs. "He says
it's like walking into a geography.
He always dreamed too much." The soapstone man
says nothing, though it's not impossible
that he might speak, having decided to,
since he appears ruthlessly objective
enough to be the image of some god.
If so, the old and unambiguous
kind who had hooves and buttocks. She won't say
what she thinks of this gift, except such things
as one must say of gifts from sons. It's plain
this hard and intimately squalid thing
shocks her. I see its gradual ascension
into the attic to be kept, forgotten.

Hitch Hikers

A thin spring rain tonight, the asphalt cold,
I passed six hitch hikers, each one alone,
rigid and melancholy by the road.
Even their upturned thumbs were still as stone.

Not one moved in petition when I came
or in derision when I passed, I thought
of Monmouth's men. The royal warning signs,
these piked devisers of some wistful plot.

In Esdraelon

In Esdraelon, twenty miles from here—
dirt road, spruce, balsam fir and poplar
and a porcupine sometimes
making you stop or steer around him—
the adults still stop
and stare after the cars of strangers,
suspiciously. But the kids
playing in dooryards and ditches
wave both hands and yell
as if they were welcoming you home.
That's strange too,
because if you stop
and try to talk to them
they act scared and cagey
and pretend to be mute,
as if they'd been caught
doing something shameful.

Purple Trilliums

These tough flowers
half-hidden
under spade-shaped, heavy leaves,
stinking like a wet cat—
so much at home
here by the lurching road.

They are not the kind
of flower one gives
to a girl, although
—aside from their stink—
they are full
of a tremulous loveliness.

But one can hardly imagine
them being picked
and put in a vase—
they belong here.

Driving to Moncton

A child turned suddenly and leapt upon
the road. My brakes shrieked out. He tumbled down
unhurt but crying wildly, with his eyes
knocked out of focus. As I drove toward town,

this troubled me, who am not heartless: fear
had been an acid in my throat, a pool
of searing bitterness. Scared witless, I
had for an instant hated that small fool.

Fireweed

Summer is not a season here;
August by the dirt road
ferns and the leaves of bushes brown as beer,
all dead, curdle the blood.

Driving Sunday through woods, I found
one stalk of fireweed, which
was the only live flower in the ground
along twelve miles of ditch.

Old Man on a Bicycle

An old man on a bicycle
    searches the ditches for beer bottles,
wearing a mackinaw in the hottest weather.
He piles the dusty green bottles
    in his knapsack, in a carton
    tied to the rear mudguard,
before he goes back he fills his pockets
if it is a good time—in the spring
or the day after a holiday.

But he doesn't complain
if it is a bad day,
if there are too few in twelve miles
to fill his knapsack.

When he finds a bottle broken
(and if there is even a crack they're no good)
he curses to himself, disgusted
with the fools who don't even know
how to throw a beer bottle
out of a car window without smashing it.

Christt

Aloft in a balsam fir I watched Christ go,
two crows in that same tree made human laughter.

He clambered over the log fence and crossed
the orange-yellow field, his purple skirts

swishing the grain and I could hear that sound,
so close he ws, and separate the hairs

in his red beard. He passed beneath me, never
once looking up, and having reached the gate

to the hill pasture shrank smaller and smaller
becoming first a fist and then a finger

and then a fleck of purple on the hillside.
At last, at the edge of the wood, he vanished
          altogether.

Hunters

Hunters, Americans in scarlet breeches,
stopping their car here, one of them goes back
to check the network of new rope that hitches
the dead black bear atop the luggage rack.
He tightens knots, looks self-conscious and proud,
even a little boyish, though it's plain
that he's not young. One senses how this cowed
and squalid beast enlivens him—its pain
and cornered anger squelched in the dark wood
that ornaments his world. It's like a child
sprung from the violent act but tamed and good,
decoratively. He can't see it wild,
alive in its own element. he might
as well have bought it and perhaps he did:
guides trap and sell them out by weight
to hunters who don't want to hunt. The dead
beast-thing secured, the car starts homeward. There
bear skins are rugs, a den is not a lair.

Grass Fires

Grass fires burn and the relentless dusk
smells like a sacrifice; the dead blades burst
open and flower as they're touched by flame,
and then are as explosively submersed
in the dark elements: the creeping ash
that always overtakes. One thinks the ram,
restless behind his wire, understands:
faggots and basins and the asherim.

The Jackers

On Christmas eve, we killed the doe,
parted her dazzled eyes, punctured her throat,
and left small scarlet trenches in the snow
where her warm blood ran out.

A thumb of brightness gouged her eyes,
a leaden hammer split her dainty head.
Grace gone, she floundered down and did not rise,
sprawled there, undone and dead.

Grief was like spoilt bread in the mouth, I bit
the pillows, though I would not eat;
lonely as God with pity for her, yet
dogged by the sweet smell of her frying meat.

Flies

Squalor is fixed in the relationship
between these flies and me, this one returning
with crazy single-mindedness to the same spot
in the precise centre of my left wrist,
feet greased with God knows what, vomit and dung,
decomposing garbage, mucus from the eyes of dead
     cats,
all this and worse — brushed off in gathering fury
and whirring back, making idiot, insistent
sounds with its wings, always coming back
to the one place on my flesh. Stung into anger
as if this fly had the same conception
of our relative positions as I,
I watch for my chance and kill him.

A small bead of my own blood
bursts from his smashed body
and glistens evilly on my stinging wrist.

Bear

At Easter we went out to kill the bear
who stole the lambs; the dogs encircled her—
our rifles stuttered, blood burst from her flesh;
her death was thunderous.

Outside a roadside diner since, I've seen
a bear cub fastened with a shining chain
whose occupation was to fascinate
stray tourists looking for a place to eat.

The Anatomy of Angels

Angels inhabit love songs. But they're sprites
not seraphim. The angel that up-ended
Jacob had sturdy calves, moist hairy armpits,
stout loins to serve the god whom she befriended,

and was adept at wrestling. She wore
a cobra like a girdle. Yet his bone
mending he spent some several tedious weeks
marking the bed they'd shared, with a great stone.

Looking for Nancy

Looking for Nancy
    everywhere, I've stopped
girls in trenchcoats
and blue dresses,
    said
Nancy I've looked
    all over
    hell for you,
Nancy I've been afraid
that I'd die
before I found you.

    But there's always
    been some mistake:

a broken streetlight,
too much rum or merely
my wanting too much
for it to be her.

Hunter, Beware

Hunter, beware this wood
    where every branch is frozen stiff for stinging.
I in my innocence thought love was peace,
    a drowsy drunkenness, a quiet singing.

Exploration: to Therese

We two exploring this, the oldest country,
the chariot afire, its foaming horses
racing each other in the same harness,

find it is not the same with us: the first
pair stumbled into it and God's eunuchs
scabbarded their blazing swords, they daft with
    wonder. He

gave them centuries to discover it,
being more patient then; for us the journey
crosses a beach between the tides, and ends.

You Said

Not even God, you said, could be so cruel
as to ignore our innermost desire:

that to escape the fixed impermanence
of all passionate things from ice to fire.

Warning to any Woman

Bluebeard, like any lover, locked one door
within the towered house he gave his bride.

My love, to make the moral clear, recall
how love became too curious and died.

Love is a Rose

Love is a rose they said. And me reborn
out of a love as arrogant as horn?
Not woman only blesses, being torn
out of herself, her time. Love is a rose is thorn.

Politicians

Miracles are physical solutions
to unembodied problems. Politicians
perceive all locks are opened with one key:
the lady's buckle broken, all the doors
breached in her lord's still room and treasury.

Therese

Therese is so small a flame
I have to cup her in my hands. Even then
if there is a wind from the north
she trembles, shrinking
down in my palms. And I'm afraid
of being burnt and dropping her
on the ground where she'll go out.

Nancy

Nancy was the smoking tines,
    the distant strawstack's blaze at night
when from my window all the dark
    closed darker on that light.

Nancy was the cool beneath
    the bridge where we were forty thieves.
Cars went over, gravel came down
    Nancy was this; and please

show me what Nancy is, I said,
    the part that can never be me.
And Nancy naked was Nancy clothed
    in denser mystery.

Biography

Out of the sea I took you, laid my mouth
against your mouth and fed you with my breath
Sea lark, imaginary girl
who now insists on being real.

Down River

In cities the embittered ones are cunning;
anguish sharpens their wits, I've seen the eye
glint in whoresons and beggars, its approach
quick and malicious as a common fly.

But here persistent misery endures;
growing thick-headed like a cow, it chews
thistles in mute protest against the rain
of innocence it cannot lose or use.

Abandoned House

The mice have left this house and swallows breed here,
flying with their peculiar jerky grace
in through the highest windows that still hold
odd glass that on clear evenings reflects
the sunset, turning all its colours lonesome
and strangely cold. And small, pink roses, once
covered with bags against the cold and patterned
around the porch, grow wild in every corner
of lawns so deep and snarled a car might cross
and not be seen. Only the smaller boys
enter this house if dared and leave on finding
everything that it's fun to break is broken.

April in New Brunswick

Spring is distrusted here, for it deceives—
snow melts upon the lawns, uncovering
last fall's dead leaves.

The Smelt Run

Smelts rot on the riverbank
there are so many
some of the men
comb them out with rakes
to prove it can be done.

They build fires
on the mudbanks at night
and get drunk fishing
with nets and jig-hooks.

They fish half the night
emptying their scoop nets
in the mud by the fires
laughing at one another.

Some of the fish
are eaten, not many,
they are small and full
of tough bones—mostly
they rot on the bank
but every night
the men come back for more.

The Deacon's Cross

The deacon's cross amid the ripened grain
sports an old coat, and cotton ribbons rain
down all around it like a festival.
The blackbirds worship there. I wish them well.

The Old People

"Next summer if I live . . ." they say,
the old people, not with dismay,
for they might add: "I'll come again
tomorrow, if it doesn't rain."

105

These Are the Men Who Live by Killing Trees

These are the men who live by killing trees—
their bones are ironwood, their muscles steel,
their faces whetstones and their hands conceal
claws hard as peavy hooks: anatomies
sectioned like the man in the Zodiac.

These are the trees: alive, the sluggish light
stationed in their moist hearts; they do not fight
the axe-blade, though they'll break an axeman's back
and look benevolent. The centuries
have made a violent marriage here, the men
wedded by violation to the trees,
so they reflect each other, taking in
strange qualities. The men assume at length
the stubborn stance of trees, their dogged strength.

St. John River

The colour of a bayonet this river
that glitters blue and solid on the page
in tourist folders, yet some thirty towns
use it as a latrine, the sewerage
seeping back to their wells, and farmers maddened
by debt or queer religions winter down
under the ice, the river bottom strewn
with heaps of decomposing bark torn loose
from pulpwood driven south, its acid juice
killing the salmon. August, when the stink
of the corrupted water floats like gas
along these streets, what most astonishes
is that the pictures haven't lied, the real
river is beautiful, as blue as steel.

Homecoming

Walking all night and always toward the wind,
thought of this house sustained me. Now I find
the porcupine-sunk porch and a wild bird
flying from room to room with cry most weird,
and all the windows blind.

New Brunswick

All breath is crystal spinning in the air,
the only warmth that strokes this friendless cold,
and winter is the season that we share,
shut out and young or shut away and old.

The very dung behind the cattle freezes,
the wind insults the face like a sprung branch,
who can condemn the exile if he seizes
an icicle and thrust it like a lance

into his heart? Oh, Christ our faith is strong
that winter lasts forever, being long.

THE THINGS WHICH ARE

Party at Bannon Brook

At the dead end of a road twisting snakelike
as that out of Eden, in a hunting camp, the hoarse creek crawling
through the closed door like the wet ghost of some drowned Adam,
coughing water on the floor, I sprawl on a straw-filled bunk
and drink rum with strangers:

> The chef in his tall white hat
> and apron embroidered
> with ribald slogans,
> spears steaks with slivers
> of white pine, roaring.

Beside me, in the leaping shadows
next the rough boards of the wall, her head
resting on a calendar from which all the months
have been ripped away, leaving only
the likeness of a woman
with orange skin and a body that might have been

stretched on a rack in the dungeon
of Gilles de Rais, it has such perverse,
blasphemous proportions, a girl sits, swaying
in time with the chef's song, her sweater
pulled out at the back, my circular arm
stroking the soft fat
of her belly—not because I love her
but because I am afraid. If we could do what we wish,
always, I would tell them I understand:
this is the season
when the bobcat is not driven away
by smoke, and the eagle
makes reconnaissance from the coast.

        But they will not listen.
        And they could do worse: tomorrow
        the chef will be cashiered, kill eight hours
        sending bills to debtors and this girl
        sit at a desk, addressing letters
        to the brains of dead men, each a packaged pudding
        shelved in cold storage, and I

in whom despair
has bred superior cunning
will escape only by long study
of how the silver beads turn to gold, falling
by my employer's window, the icicles
stroked by an amorous sun.

The Terror of
Thinking Myself No More a Poet

If I came in
no more a poet

because the crows
that continually press
had at last eaten up
every seed in my field
every scrap of my flesh.

I'd die, I said,
I'd cut with a knife,
I'd cut off the wick
with a blunt knife.

You'd live, she said.
You'd want to die,
you'd not kill yourself.
I know you too well
you like lager beer
and abhor Jack Knife.
And besides
you'll have me
for the rest of your life.

Ugh! Writing poems
I've smoked two cigarettes at once!
Would you want to lie
by a skeleton, every shred
of my flesh licked off by the crows!
I'd live, she said.

But bones in your bed!
White bones, and later

yellow bones in your bed!
Such bones as would scratch and tear
and a skull for a head, I said!
An eyeless, noseless, earless, hairless, brainless
skull in your bed!

Then we'd wear my flesh.
I don't know about poetry.
But I recognize everybody
in every one of your poems, she said.

Disguise

This is the amazing thing
that it is so easy
to fool them—
the sane bastards.

I can talk
about weather, eat,
preside at meetings
of the PTA.
They don't know.

Me foreign as a Martian.
With the third eye in my forehead!
But I comb my hair
cleverly so it doesn't show

except a little
sometimes when the wind blows.

Black Thread

My sister sewed her hand,
the soft flesh of her palm,
black thread under the skin,
the starbright needle
pricking her skin
so that I itched
wherever it went in.

She broke the thread in her teeth
and laughed in my face. The thread
dangling down from her flesh.
I shut both eyes with my fists
counting each stitch in her flesh.

Counting each stitch in her flesh
while she laughed and laughed like a witch.

Salvation

"Are you saved, brother?"
asks the Baptist preacher.
"Are you saved, like me?"

Ah, my poor brother!
I would touch your eyes with my spit,
if you were strong enough
and if that would open them.

I had no choice.
Sometimes, I even wish
He had let me go—

flowers spring up
where the blood pours from my side,

but I have nightmares
in which I relive
those days and nights in the tomb.

Strange Flowers

These flowers are beautiful enough.
Soft-eyed and moist
on their wiry bush.

But I don't know their name. . .
and some bushes burn!

Sheepish, I stand
at the fence and look.

Fire

The fire runs as fast as a man.
The swift beasts run ahead:
rabbit and deer and fox and lynx.
The lumbering ones are dead.

Smoke travels slowly, yet it came
into town weeks before the flame.
Now the beasts enter, frantic feet
racing the fire down the street.

The fire slows. Concrete and stone.
Beasts stop. They breathe again:
rabbit and deer and fox and lynx
with arm's reach of men.

Drunk: Falling

Everybody sees
the drunk lose his grip
on the wet black bricks,
the soggy mackinaw
slide over his head,
limp knees
slipping through
oil-scummed puddles
to the sharp pavement.

But look again.
You'll notice
the terrible dignity
with which he prolongs
his descent:

Saul dying,
Achilles to Lycaon:
ah, friend, seeing thou too must die
why thus lamentest thou?

The Mark

The mark is on me.
As I approach the liquor store
the winos emerge from the alley
thrust out their quivering palms,
like cripples accosting Christ.

And I give them money:
a quarter for a pint of beer,
ten cents toward a shot of rum.
"You know what it's like", they say.
"You know what it's like".

Imagining the taste,
the cool of it on the tongue.
Oh, God, the first
little glimmer of warmth
in the stomach, and then

the stones softening, the flutes,
the incorruptible body,
Marsyas challenging Apollo—

yes, brothers,
I know what it's like.
I know.

Novelty Booth

I'd gotten under the canvas
to get out of the rain
but I had to buy something

so I grabbed the first thing
I saw—a glass flower,

the kind they sell
at cheap carnivals
from here to Florida.

I picked mine apart
with my fingernails

and inside
there was a tiny cup
like a thimble

full of pus and blood
(I thought I must be going crazy)

and when I poured it out
(this is the part
you'll never believe)

there was another flower!

And this one
was
made of rubies
and diamonds
and all the jewels
whose names I'm
too poor to remember.

I should have stopped there.
But I pried it open
and the pieces rolled under
the feet of the crowd
waiting for the freak show, and

there was nothing left
except a smaller thimble

and when I spilled it
a flower like the first;
you could buy a dozen for a nickle.

The rain has stopped. The crowds are gone.
"The show's over, Mac.
Be a good fellow and go home".

It is almost morning.
I stand here shredding flowers.
My hands stink,
drip pus and blood.

November 11

There was blood.
"His buttons shone
like six little suns
of polished brass.
under the heels
of his looking glass boots,
little red flowers
sprang out of the grass".

No, there was blood.
"And Reverend Death came like a padre
and laid his hand
on his shoulder and quoted—"

No. There was pus—don't you understand?
On the third day my belly bloated
and the other guys
couldn't stand the smell
and—"The sky was as blue
as the plumed helmet
of a grenadier.
All firing ceased.
The only sounds
were the sad choirboy voice of a bugle
and the whisper of the air".

The Bull Moose

Down from the purple mist of trees on the mountain,
lurching through forests of white spruce and cedar,
stumbling through tamarack swamps,
came the bull moose
to be stopped at last by a pole-fenced pasture.

Too tired to turn or, perhaps, aware
there was no place left to go, he stood with the cattle.
They, scenting the musk of death, seeing his great head
like the ritual mask of a blood god, moved to the other end
of the field, and waited.

The neighbours heard of it, and by afternoon
cars lined the road. The children teased him
with alder switches and he gazed at them
like an old, tolerant collie. The women asked
if he could have escaped from a Fair.

The oldest man in the parish remembered seeing
a gelded moose yoked with an ox for plowing.
The young men snickered and tried to pour beer
down his throat, while their girl friends took their pictures.

And the bull moose let them stroke his tick-ravaged flanks,
let them pry open his jaws with bottles, let a giggling girl
plant a little purple cap
of thistles on his head.

When the wardens came, everyone agreed it was a shame
to shoot anything so shaggy and cuddlesome.
He looked like the kind of pet
women put to bed with their sons.

So they held their fire. But just as the sun dropped in the river
the bull moose gathered his strength
like a scaffolded king, straightened and lifted his horns
so that even the wardens backed away as they raised their rifles.
When he roared, people ran to their cars. All the young men
leaned on their automobile horns as he toppled.

Comparison

Comparing pigs with cattle, Jack the butcher
says he likes cows and understands them. They
go where they're sent and stand until they're struck
by his great hammer, then bleed drowsily.

Pigs, on the other hand, disgust him: running,
darting and leaping and befouling him
with blood that spurts out of their backs because
they won't accept the axe like gentlemen.

The Cat

On a cloth mat
under the crackling stove,
the cat loafs on his belly,
laps milk from a china plate.

Beads of blue snow
from the other side
of the frozen river
still cling to his fur.

At intervals, the wind
rattles the storm door
and he stiffens
and shies away,
one eye bright, the other
a hideous crust of blood and pus.

The Shack Dwellers

Most of them look
as though their bodies were boneless.

Every animal
has its own defense:
theirs is plasticity.

Kick them in the face
and nothing breaks.
It's as if your boot
sank in wet dough.

But sometimes a trick
of hunger or heredity
gives one small bones
like an aristocrat's,
transparent skin
and delicate, blue veins.

You'll see one of the lost
Bourbons or Romanoffs,
dirty toes protruding
from the holes in his sneakers,
a hint of the old
hauteur in his hawk nose
as he tries to talk the grocer
out of a roll of bologna
and a loaf of stale bread.

Stoney Ridge Dance Hall

They don't like strangers.
So be careful how you smile.

Eight generations
of Hungerfords, McGards and Staceys
have lived on this ridge
like incestuous kings.
Their blood is so pure
it will not clot.

This is the only
country they know.
There are men here
who have never heard of Canada.

When they tire of dancing
they go down the road
and drink white lightning
out of the bung
of a molasses puncheon.

But they never forget
to strap on the knuckles
they've made from beer bottle
caps and leather

and there are sharp spikes
in their orange logging boots.

The Gift

Like the spluttering wick
of a dry coal oil lamp,
the day begins.

Hump-backed with cold,
the shack woman gathers
fresh twigs—the gift
of last night's raw,
wall-piercing wind.

Francis

A wool stocking-cap and a flannel-lined
windbreaker,
the buttons all different,
fastened up to his throat,

> and the sun
> like slivers of dry wood
> in the flesh, this
> third week of July—

Francis laughs at me, his teeth
so yellow and blunt
he might chew roots
like a bear, laughs in my face,
Ha!
what keeps out the cold, she'll keep out the heat, he says.

The East Brighton Road

Horseflies at suck in moist yellow sores
on her sunk back, the raw-boned mare
tugs at the clattering waggon, stuck
in the tenacious clay, a weakness
more stubborn than any strength
driving her clay-caked neck
into its ruptured collar.

The old man,
whose body might have been hewn
out of cat spruce with a dull axe,
squats in the box, intent
on her struggle, but not
interfering, his eyes half-shut,
unmoved, the reins lax
in his left hand, his tongue
solemn around an ice cream cone.

Money

My sister writes from Halifax.
"Dear Bruddie..."
Sure enough, she wants money.

Money! Why she and I
had been reared naked
were clothes money—
teeth coins ours had been knocked out,
eyes dollars hers and mine
snipped off with a razor.

Breakfast was dollar bills
sprinkled with ground dimes
washed down with melted pennies
brown as coffee, but richer, sugared
with silver—if we had any.

As I remember it, our house
was roofed in banknotes woven together.
Rain blew in on my bed. The roof leaked.
Father said: there's no money.

"Dear Bruddie..."
Sistie wants money.
She and I
write baby talk about money:
"Don't be silly, we wore
gold, azure and purple underpants
because papa stole
that cloth from the cotton mill,
flour bag shirts and madeover pants and dresses.
We ate beans until they came out of our ears
and mama saved even the salt from her tears.

But, p.s., I need money".

Fired

At five, convinced to fire meant to throw,
I saw The Company affix steel dogs
and chain men's legs and winch them up like logs
for heaving from the millyard. Then they flew—
across the sawdust dunes and lumber racks,
over shrill saws, stunned men and startled horses,
over the roofs of boxcars, till their courses
ending, their legs released, they fell in stacks.

The Stenographer

She long ago
gave up
dreaming
of freedom.

But, sometimes,
when the boss is out,
she closes her eyes
for a moment
and imagines

the office overrun
by Circassian slavers.

They strip her naked.
Her chains and collar
are of solid gold.

And the auctioneer
whose whip counts
bids on her buttocks
looks exactly
like Errol Flynn.

The Grove Beyond the Barley

This grove is too secret: one thinks of murder.
Coming upon your white body (for as yet
I do not know you, therefore have no right
to speak of discovering
you, can address myself
to your body only) seeing the disorder
of your naked limbs, the arms outstretched
like one crucified, the legs bent like a runner's,
it took me less than a second to write a novel:
the husband in the black suit
worn at his wedding, the hired man
in his shirt the colour
of a rooster's comb and, in the end, you
thrown here like an axed colt.
Then I saw your breasts: they are not asleep,
move like the shadows of leaves
stirred by the wind. I hope you do not waken,
before I go; one who chooses
so dark a place
to lie naked
might cry out. The shadows quicken,
I wish you a lover,
dreams of sunlit meadows,
imagine myself a gentle satyr.

At the Drug Store

The hands of the boy kneeling at the magazine rack
do not sweat or falter though one almost touches
a thigh and the other reaches slowly for a naked breast.

Her answer is always a pout of anticipation.
She poses no nervous riddles, no sharp surprises,
will refuse him nothing, ask for nothing he cannot give.

Eyes incredulous, as at the first crest of passion,
he stirs but will not look up as, half on purpose,
girls, full-fleshed and whispering, brush awkwardly against him.

Canticle

May-white, the young girl's legs appear
stark, and unnaturally bare.
Six months estranged, the naked sun
feels curiously alien,

and the spring wind that makes the grass
caress her heels, libidinous:
however hoydenish the stride,
the limbs of an embarrassed bride.

In time, like a long-married man
the sun will rest his hand upon
this flesh habitually, seem
to think of something else, or dream.

And soon the wind-blown grass will rise
familiarly, to stroke her thighs.
But, for the moment, these address
themselves to their own nakedness.

Flesh as vulnerable as snow
and as unseasonable, aglow
with eagerness and yet afraid
in its athletic masquerade.

For all I know, her mind may feel
no more than the mechanical
rhythm of muscles and take in
only the climate of her skin.

Child of her time in gabardine
shorts and no Shunemite May Queen.
Of this I'm sure: the body knows
itself exposed from hips to toes,

shrinks back, attempting to withdraw
from weather masculine and raw;
its secret, in these vernal streets
revealed to everyone it meets.

All this will pass with the Maypole,
the self be comfortably whole.
In the meantime, she leaps, expels
unease in adolescent yells.

Porch

Immersed in night, my senses sharpen, hear
the nervous splash of water that can't stop
falling, but hesitates before each drop
breaks in a porcelain basin and the ear.

Moonlight flows through the oilcloth, a sheen
upon each grain of dust descending from
the fuliginous ceiling, platinum
stars woven in the window like a screen.

Our bodies touch, each meeting separate:
her arm, distinct and compact, like a cat
soft on my shoulder, while both ankles strain
against mine, bone to bone, her drowsing breast
crowding me toward the wall, passion at rest—
and the dull pressure of beginning pain.

October Snow Storm

The fallen snow
is green, because of the grass.
It is as though I walked
through the crystal
of an emerald.

There is so much
on the leaves
of the Manitoba maple,
its limbs bend
like foam from a fountain.

And the purple dahlias,
all but their faces
hidden,
lay their heads
on their shoulders and grieve
like flowers in a fairy tale.

Nightpiece

Like all the people whom I know
    or most, at any rate,
tomorrow I shall wake and go
    out to a job I hate.

This is November and I wish
    I were a simple bird,
could live on fruit white as the flesh
    of the thrice-risen Lord.

From my window across the street
    mornings at work, I see
a lawn where sparrows pluck and eat
    the winterberry tree.

The Execution

On the night of the execution
a man at the door
mistook me for the coroner.
"Press", I said.

But he didn't understand. He led me
into the wrong room
where the sheriff greeted me:
"You're late, Padre".

"You're wrong", I told him. "I'm Press".
"Yes, of course, Reverend Press".
We went down a stairway.

"Ah, Mr. Ellis", said the Deputy.
"Press!" I shouted. But he shoved me
through a black curtain.
The lights were so bright
I couldn't see the faces
of the men sitting
opposite. But, thank God, I thought
they can see me!

"Look!", I cried. "Look at my face!
Doesn't anybody know me?"

Then a hood covered my head.
"Don't make it harder for us", the hangman whispered.

Explanation

My best poems
don't get written,
because I'm still scared.

Don't laugh: the reports of people
who've seen the Cherubim
differ, but all agree
they're terrible beasts: part ox, part eagle, part lion;

yet even Leonardo
was afraid to paint them
as other than
quaintly winged babies.

Fruit of the Hurricane

Above the rain, above the roar of the wind
come rampaging from the Caribbean,
between the times when limbs crack like pistol shots,
we can hear the apples, thousands of them,
hitting the wet floor of the orchard as hard as hooves.

Here, sheltered, it would be pleasant to think of them:
a rain of apples, apples so sweet and moist
we might quench our thirst if water never fell again;
great heaps of apples, yellow and red,
apples rolled along the ground by tomorrow's wind.

But, in the morning, we will have to begin to gather them,
quickly, before they rot. We will need all our strength.

Better we go to bed.

The Genealogy of Morals

Take any child dreaming of pickled bones
Shelved in a coal-dark cellar understairs
(we are all children when we dream) the stones
red-black with blood from severed jugulars.

Child Francis, Child Gilles went down those stairs,
returned sides, hands and ankles dripping blood,
Bluebeard and gentlest saint. The same nightmares
instruct the evil, as inform the good.

The Chopper

His axe blade nearing
the red pine's heart,

the chopper strikes harder,
doesn't hear or see

the hysterical squirrel
on the topmost limb

running nowhere and back
faster and faster.

Trans-Canada Highway

The black girls run with their pails of hot coals
because it is raining hard and if they don't get home soon
they'll have nothing but soggy cinders—

rain ricochets like tracer bullets in a newsreel;
as they sprint over the hills,
mushrooms of steam
burst from each swinging pail.

The Drunken Poet

Sometimes, when he got drunk and came back late,
he stopped a moment before every door
in the dark hallway of the boarding house,
like an intrusive saint, or murderer.

And he knew everything that those within
slept with, they laughed and whimpered in their sleep,
and he had half a mind to blackmail them
and half a mind to cover them and weep.

Later, in his own room, he seized a pen
and paper, set down everything he knew,
and re-united God and devil, since
he shared all secrets common to the two.

Each time he laughed he tasted salt. Each tear
tickled him still he howled. He went to bed,
the papers in his hand, awoke too sick
to go to work and burned them all, unread.

Voyeur

Each night in his dark furnished room, he kneels
opposite an open window till she comes,
haloed, under Orion and reveals
herself in gold and young chrysanthemums.

Or so he phrases it; seeing her bare,
remembers Swinburne and the two Rossettis;
winces observing that she's had her hair
shortened again, deplores her vulgar panties.

The Eloi and the Morlocks

At the edge of the field
behind the tarpapered shacks,
grow wild roses so delicate
their petals are jarred
loose by the lightest step.

The field stretches
to the end of the earth:
in the west its golden green
joins the silver blue of the sky.

Golden green? Silver blue?
When one can't walk without trampling
orange or purple flowers
and the sun is blinding red?
On so bright a day
one daren't look
at more than one
colour at a time.

The squatters
venture no farther
than ther murky doorways.
Against the darkness, I see white hands
shielding white faces.

And the moles
burrow deeper
in fear of the sun.

The Idolator

Perhaps, we should not know our God too well.
They say a man cut his own face in stone,
then set that idol up and bowed him down,
while God walked every day in Israel.

And God, roaring with anger, called him out
and slew his sons and his camel and daughter,
powdered the idol and mixed it with water
and dog's blood, poured the message down his throat.

God's fingers opening his mouth, God's breath
panting into his face, he swallowed stone.
And all the people watched, paler than death,
then left to make them idols of their own.

Aleister Crowley

In my boy's cave of dreaming before sleep,
a ladder dangled in a darksome well,
and, at its foot, doors opened to a keep
where the concordances of daytime fell.

King of Two Sicilies and Priest of Thoth,
I bested pythons and the shambling dead,
swaggered barefoot on naked Ashtaroth,
was flagellated, love-chained to her bed.

Keats speaks of it, young Gilbert Chesterton
returned with sketches, later burnt; most men
stop all the doors with dirt; the moonstruck Crowley
fed live birds to a skeleton and cut
himself with actual knives till, having brought
it up, he purchased bricks and built an abbey.

Sometimes

Sometimes, not often, I wish there were only
the clean rapture of the body. I wish I could go
into a strange place, an amnesiac, and find that she too
had forgotten history
                        Oh, love is good
but it reaches out
to take in the stars,
runs backwards and forwards. Sometimes I wish
for a world no bigger than the coupling bodies
of two clockless strangers.
                        But when I seek it,
she makes some small gesture—puts her hand to her hair—and I can tell
she has not forgotten herself, that she tries to please me
for some purpose of her own, and I almost weep; or she murmurs
some private word, and I curse myself and berate her.

Bird of Prey

All secrets spoken, her ravenous mouth
whispers "I love you", this over and over,
pleads as before that cold refuser, death,
that I put on the body of her lover.

Each repetition is more desperate,
starved beyond tenderness for self or me,
with every word of adoration, hate
attacks this object more ravenously.

"I love you", she says and each syllable
claws at my back, its black wings pitiless;
"I love you" and again the scalding, cruel
beak thrusts and tears, maddened and murderous.

"I love you" and because it is not I
she loves, would torment me and have me die.

Love Poem for Therese

We asked too much
of one another,

broken, looked
to the broken for wholeness.

That truth we shared today.

And this also: perhaps, there is no one.
Perhaps all are broken: three billion dolls
leaking sawdust. Heat, light and power
shut off in the forgotten warehouse.

No wonder, you threw yourself in my arms and wept!
No wonder, I whispered all
the old love names as I clung to you.

Waiting for Her

Waiting for her,
rain on the windshield,
cars passing,
their tires hissing
on the black pavement;

one minute the rain
pounding the car roof
as drummers
must have pounded
their drums at old executions,
with their fists,
not wanting to hear the screams;

the next minute
so quiet
I can hear my cigarette
burning when I inhale.

I listen
for her, I know how
she walks at night
and in the rain, with a different rhythm.

I brace myself to pretend
if she comes I was sure she'd come,
if she doesn't that I don't care.

Dancer

The sun is horizontal, so the flesh
of the near-naked girl bouncing a ball
is netted in its light, an orange mesh
weaving between her and the shadowed wall.

Her body glistening and snake-crescendoes
electric in her lighted muscles, she
pauses before each pitch, then rears and throws
the ball against the darkness, venomously.

The interlocking stones cry out and hurl
the black globe back, all human purpose stript
from its wild passage, and the bouncing girl
bolts in and out of darkness after it.

Stumbling in the shadows, scalded blind
each time she whirls to face the sunlight, she
at last restores the pattern of her mind.
But every ball's more difficult to see.

Fall

Young boys in white hoods
hurl handfuls of the first snow

at the few rust-coloured leaves
still clutching the tip
of the highest limb
of the sugar maple.

Picking Raspberries

Noon.
But it is twilight
here
inside the
raspberry thicket:
green-black leaves
dull and nail-tipped
arrows of the sun
so they caress.

We won't feel the thorns
for hours yet;
tonight,
I will bathe
the hot scars
on her back and legs
with cool liquids. Now

the sweet berries
break
apart
on our tongues.

Moon Fear

One of the secret thoughts that go as soon
as they're put into words: I saw the moon
rise from a valley on the other side
of the black hills and burn with orange fire
over rockpiles, gaunt spruces and barbed wire,
and thought I'd never seen a moon so wide
or bright or low; for an instant, I went
back into childhood, fearing that it swelled
with God's wrath or an evil element,
shivered with horror until I expelled
held-breath in laughter, curiously glad
of the brief and unworldly fright I'd had.

Jane at Two

Lifted to the night window, Jane
(mark how detached, yet curious, her eyes)
starts at quickgold created in the pane,
grabs for the moon—and misses it—and cries!

Three Choices

Having been flogged with belts, not short of bleeding,
badgered by books and flayed by tongues like nettles,
I had three choices: madness, death or verse,
each of which asks more questions than it settles.

Closing Time

Night falling, the all-day rain
turns to hail, the puddles to slush,
yet the sober drunks
without even enough
for one last beer
gather opposite the liquor store
to watch the blue-smocked man
whose hand's on the bolt
of the fluorescent door.

The ice pellets beat
at their up-turned faces
as their eyes, with his,
follow the electric hands
of the clock suspended
above the shelves
of sparkling bottles.

Storm

This is the wildest
night of the winter.

But the cat lying,
paws folded under,
on the open verandah rail,
doesn't seem to notice

except she half-closes
her eyes each time
the howling wind
throws sleet in her face.

In Peace

"It is not death that frightens me", she said,
turning away to watch a waterfall
of moonlight drench the marble. "No", she frowned,
it is not death, it is not death at all".

What then?
          "You'll laugh at me".
                         I never laugh.
"Don't ask me to put things for which no words
have been discovered into other words".
Without such trickery, we could not talk.
"We talk too much", she said, shaking the moon
out of her hair, one finger following
the marble lettering:
                  ". . . in peace".
                            In peace.
All of our lives are spent in seeking peace
and when it comes we fight like jig-hooked eels.
"You said you never laughed".
                         No words again!
"I don't feel quite right about laughter—here".
Is that part of the secret thing you fear?

"Perhaps, but it's no secret really. Only
I don't think we should seem so happy . . ."

Because they'll hate us?
                    "You make it sound—"
Because they'll hate us?
                       "Yet, I suppose that's it".
Listen, before we go, I'll curse you, then
you can lie down and weep so that they'll hear!

"You're mocking me!"
                         Just being helpful.
                                        "No,
I heard the rhythm of your words. You know
how when you listen to one instrument
within an orchestra the others fade
as though the listener played all by ear.
I heard your hatred then. You have a way
of hiding whips in jokes".
                         And you're a fool
or maybe looking for some way to make
your hatred enter me so you can have
hate's satisfactions and love's vanity:
a woman's favourite trick against a man.

"I want to go now".
                         Do you still think they'll hate us?
"I want to go now".
                         Wait for a moment and we'll watch the moon
walk like a ghost trailing its dead-white shroud
up that great silver ramp to the black cloud.

the cloud were death's ship taking back a spy.
Did you ever mark how many qualities
the moon shares with a ghost?
                         "I want to go now".

Psalm

Through a kaleidoscope of spray and sun,
a hose whirling on the lawn, a circle of children
in rainbow swim suits, making their own music,
heads thrown back, chanting, light streaming from their bodies!

Wishing I could join them, I think of the laughing Jesus
of the Acts of John, how he linked the hands
of his disciples, made them dance in circles.
"You who dance not, know not what we are knowing".
"Dance, dance, thus, thus, whole and happy for Our Lord St. John".

Daisies

We walked a mile from the road, and with every step
she broke off a daisy, till she held thousands
in a great bunch against her chest,

till they covered her face and her red-gold pigtails,
till the top of her head was the eye of a daisy;
she sniffed of them, tasted their petals and pulp,
felt their heads and stalks with her cheeks and fingers.

That soil was rich, had we walked all day
she could have kept counting her steps with daisies:
running back to the car, she threw open her arms
and her body burst like a fountain of flowers.

Canadian Love Song

Your body's a small word with many meanings.
Love. If. Yes. But. Death.
Surely I will love you a little while,
perhaps as long as I have breath.

December is thirteen months long,
July's one afternoon; therefore,
lovers must outwit wool,
learn how to puncture fur.

To my love's bed, to keep her warm,
I'll carry wrapped and heated stones.
That which is comfort to the flesh
is sometimes torture to the bones.

FIVE NEW BRUNSWICK POETS

Communion: 1946 and 1962

Through the forest path on the ridge,
down the dug road to the swamp where the herons rest,
a young hostage prince sketched by El Greco
in denim shorts and a sweat shirt. He squats in the grass,
dreaming of Peru, watching the great birds and the river
winding to the west where steam roars from its cataracts
spilt on the sun, squats there and waits for me
to stir in the hill cedars and the hot cells
of his palpitant body. . . .

> *When I am a man I will not be afraid*
> *of the stirring in the cedars, the heat in my body.*
> *When I am a man I will come into my kingdom.*
> *When I am a man I will not be afraid.*

Oh, little one, my lost Dauphin,
my Czarevitch, my last of the Bonapartes;
I followed mirages and was all but maddened
by thirst and the tittering skulls.
They offered drink, and I stopped.

> *What if the man I will be came from the cedars?*
> *I would flee, crying. What if the river*
> *Extinguished the sun?*

Little one, I would weep
for you, but that were self-pity.

> *I will go home now.*
> *Night birds I cannot name*
> *Make evil sounds in the cedars.*
> *When I am a man I will not be afraid.*

The Walking Dead

The dead rise and shuffle toward me, reach out for my hand,
greet me with that faint sneer, that stare of disbelief
with which men meet death; I have come to expect this,
no longer cringe or cry out, though I watch for hours
in the stink — no, not of disintegration, but of chemicals,
alcohol, formaldehyde — grip the claws of thousands,
all dead, all cheating death of its only beauty:
decay, and the final cleanliness
of earth, air, fire, water — their only passion,
fear of the morticians who'll wrestle them, screaming,
into their element-proof lead coffins.

Anti-Narcissus

My own face —
bloated and green
but my own face
pulsating like a
Lovecraft god in
the salt grass under
this muddy water!

I can't tear my eyes away.

Christ, but I wish
I knew the direction
a man had to take
to keep from meeting
himself.

This spring
it's gotten so bad
I see my own
bitter lips and eyes
growing into
the Buddha face
of the moon.

Night of Storm

After each silence, I hear the storm
gather its strength in the snowbound thicket
northwest of the river (in the dark, sleepless
I time it to daytime things), hear it howl
over black-white ice, bound the open fallow,
clamber the ridge, thrash, falter and stammer
in a tangle of beech, yellow birch and maple,
break free and attack this house, lunge at these doors
till they almost give, then, as if on signal
sink under the sills and whimper, shrink to a groan
on the porch steps, die at the cellar windows —
where the breath pauses in my throat and chest
as though (and this amazes me)
I were ready to pity the wind.

Railway Waiting Room, Truro, Nova Scotia

I don't even know what language he speaks,
but since 3 a.m. he's given up trying
to make the cop understand
where he was going,
and he can't find his ticket,
if he ever had one. Getting hotter and louder,
the cop names cities:
'Montreal?' 'Regina?' 'Winnipeg?' 'Toronto?'
and the little round foreigner
only cries harder.

The Migrant Hand

For how many thousands of years, for how many millions
of baskets and waggonloads and truckloads of onions,
or cotton, or turnips has this old man knelt
in the dirt of sun-crazy fields? If you ask him,
he'll put you off: he's suspicious of questions.
The truth is that Adam, a day out of Eden,
started him gathering grapes: old Pharoah
sold him to Greece; he picked leeks for the Seljuks,
garlic for Tuscans, Goths and Normans,
pumpkins and maize for the Pilgrim Fathers,
has forgotten them all, forgotten all of the past, except
the last ten hours of blackflies and heat,
the last two hundred barrels of potatoes.

Wasp

A wasp on the wrong side
of my parked car's windshield — a thorned phallus
stuttering like a machine gun, black and golden —
striped on the passive pane. In sudden pity
for him, myself and every other being
beating at unseen walls, and fearing his
sting like a sizzling awl, since I've been stung,
I try to rescue and expel him, not
certain which aim is paramount. A book
threatening to break his back by accident,
I swish a leafy, resilient alder branch
after, over and under him, conceiving
he fears it as a man instinctively
fears giant winged things. Though that things fly
shouldn't astonish wasps as it does me.
But he jumps sideways and drops out of reach
inside the defroster, yammering!
His beautiful, masculine body gone
crazy with pitiless confusion.
Motor and fan switched on, he's
blown back still stubbornly probing
the windshield, his fish-scale wings roaring,
his hed held down like a drill.
I scoop with the alder,
once, twice, a hundred times. Still he eludes me —
as the glass eludes him. What can I do with him?
Ignore of kill him? Accept defeat?
Suddenly, now, it's ridiculously important
that this bug escape his predicament
and not escape me. Holding my breath,
I grab him with my bare fingers and hurl him out —
out through the open door! Like a hot coal
grasped in the naked hand!
                              Foolishly happy,
exhausted, licking my sore paw like a dog,
I sit here, thinking of glass
and the jokes it plays in the world.

Edna

She's got the right eyes
and the separate laughs,
the silly, on-purpose one
she gives to adults,
the wise, just-happens one
she keeps to herself.

Too bad God
in letting her be eight forever
didn't remember
to stop all the clocks
at the same time

so that instead of
those mildewed ropes
bursting out of
elastic stockings

she had hopscotch legs
that go in all directions
at once,
and the funny kind of beauty
we try to meet
with gentle laughter.

R.E. Balch was born in England in 1894 and came to Canada in 1913. The following year he joined the Canadian Field Artillery and spent what he describes with characteristic accuracy as three "lousy years" in the trenches. In 1923 he received a B.Sc. in Agriculture from the Ontario Agricultural College, and acquired both the M.Sc. and Ph.D degrees from Syracuse University before becoming head of the Dominion Entomology Laboratory in Fredericton in 1929 and pursuing a distinguished career as an entomologist and ecologist.

His photographs reflect a seventy-year interest in Canadian farmers, woodsmen, and fishermen and in the sustaining life of their homes and families. For the past forty-five years that interest has been centred upon rural New Brunswick in particular.

Index of First Lines

A

B

C

D

54 Darkness, the smell of earth, the smell of apples

105 The deacon's cross amid the ripened grain

170 The dead rise and shuffle toward me, reach out for my hand

12 Dearest of strangers: in your separate room

127 Down from the purple mist of trees on the mountain

E

149 Each night in his dark furnished room, he kneels

29 Elizabeth, in your shoes with tartan laces

53 Emptied from Eden, I look down

63 Every five minutes they turn

122 Everybody sees

F

140 The fallen snow

62 Father, she says, was handsome as a Spaniard

121 The fire runs as fast as a man

61 Five dogs, bitch-crazed in the dying mustard

30 Five laths in a cotton dress

174 For how many thousands of years, for how many millions

74 For twenty-five cents

53 From that they found most lovely, most abhorred

68 The Fynch cows poisoned

G

79 Georgie and Fenwick Cranston

67 A girl, fifteen perhaps

26 God, I have sought you as a fox seeks chickens

47 God sour the milk of the knacking wench

94 Grass fires burn and the relentless dusk

17 A gushing carrousel, the cock

H

I

J

K

L

M

N

O

P

Q-R

S

T

U-V-W

X-Y